This book
belongs to

_____

This educational book was created in cooperation with Children's Television Workshop, producers of SESAME STREET. Children do not have to watch the television show to benefit from this book. Workshop revenues from this book will be used to help support CTW educational projects.

ON MY WAY WITH SESAME STREET

Volume 3

Getting Ready for School

Featuring the Sesame Street Characters

Children's Television Workshop/Funk & Wagnalls

Authors

Emily Perl Kingsley
Michaela Muntean
Patricia Relf

Illustrators

Tom Cooke
A. Delaney
Tom Leigh
Joe Mathieu
Maggie Swanson

Copyright © 1989 Children's Television Workshop. Sesame Street puppet characters © 1989 Jim Henson Productions, Inc. All rights reserved under the International and Pan-American Copyright Conventions. Sesame Street®, the Sesame Street sign®, and On My Way with Sesame Street are trademarks and service marks of Children's Television Workshop. Published in the United States of America by Western Publishing Company, Inc., Racine, WI 53404, in conjunction with Children's Television Workshop. Distributed by Funk & Wagnalls, Mahwah, N.J. Manufactured in the United States of America.

0-8343-0077-X   6 7 8 9 0

A Parents' Guide to
GETTING READY FOR SCHOOL

This book is designed to help children make the transition from home to school by teaching them what happens during a typical school day. Children feel more comfortable entering new situations when they know what to expect.

In GETTING READY FOR SCHOOL, you can take your children through the school day with ''Off to School,'' ''School Work,'' ''Lunchtime,'' ''Music Class,'' ''On the Playground,'' and ''Clean Up Time.''

''Show and Tell'' is often a favorite part of the school day and on Sesame Street it can be hilarious.

A special part of the school year is the school play. ''Super Grover and the Three Bears'' is a funny story in which your child will love taking part.

We hope the stories and activities in this book will help your children feel more confident as they approach their first day of school.

**The Editors
SESAME STREET BOOKS**

Off to School!

Big Bird is walking to school.
Take him there on the green path.

Bert is riding the school bus to school.
Take him there on the yellow path.

Betty Lou is riding her bicycle to school.
Take her there on the red path.

Prairie Dawn is riding in a car to school.
Take her there on the blue path.

Big Bird Follows the Signs

"Hi, Betty Lou," said Big Bird. "Can you tell me how to get to the school? Prairie Dawn is playing in the school orchestra and I have to take her cello to her."

"Go down that way, Big Bird," Betty Lou answered. "Then just follow the signs. But you'd better hurry. It's almost time for the concert."

Big Bird stopped at the corner. "Oh, look! There's a sign that says DON'T WALK. Betty Lou said to follow the signs, so I'd better not walk."

"Wow! Here's my stop. That sign says TO THE STREET."
Big Bird jumped up and ran out of the subway.

"What a silly sign! It says ONE WAY,"
said Big Bird. "Anybody knows I can only
walk one way!"

"This sign says STOP, so I'm stopping.
But, gee, I wonder how long I have to stop here."

"Oh, this sign says GO TEAM GO! Now I can go!" said Big Bird.

"Here's another sign. It says NO LEFT TURN! I guess that means I should go straight."

"Here's the school! But that sign says SLOW – SCHOOL ZONE. I'd better slow down."

"Hurry up, Big Bird," called Prairie Dawn. "The concert's about to begin."

"There are so many signs," said Big Bird. "I wonder if there's one that says SLEEP. Boy, am I tired!"

flag

chalkboard

plant

clock

good
morning

chalk

easel

teacher

eraser

brushes

chair

globe

apple

desk

student

wastebasket

clay

modeling stick

Big Bird at School

Big Bird is painting a picture of one of his friends. Can you tell who it is?

School Work

Book, bell, and boat.
Which word rhymes with goat?
Point to the picture
of the boat.

Two, top, and ten.
Which word rhymes with hen?
Point to the picture
of the thing that rhymes with hen.

Soap, scissors, sun.
Which word rhymes with fun?
Point to the picture
of the thing that rhymes with fun.

Mop, man, and mat.
Which word rhymes with hat?
Point to the picture
of the thing that rhymes with hat.

SHOW
AND
TELL

It was Show and Tell Day at school. Everyone brought something special to show to the class during Show and Tell time. Betty Lou hid hers in her cubby hole.

Bert put a big box in his cubby. He wouldn't tell anyone what was inside. "I want it to be a surprise," he said.

"Come on, Bert," said Betty Lou. "Let's help Herry." Herry Monster was building a block castle. Nearby, Grover was reading a book and Ernie was making a clay animal.

Soon everyone gathered around the teacher.
"Psst, Betty Lou!" Bert whispered. "Is it Show and Tell time?"
"Not yet, Bert," said Betty Lou. "It's story time."
Bert had trouble keeping his mind on the story the teacher read to the class. He was thinking about his Show and Tell surprise.

After the story, everyone sat down at a table.

"Oh, boy," Bert said. "Now it's Show and Tell time!"

"No, Bert," Betty Lou said. "Now it's time to paint."

Bert was disappointed, but Betty Lou loved to paint. She made a picture of a beautiful bird.

When they were finished, they washed their hands and put their paints away. Bert cleaned up faster than anyone else.

At last everyone was ready for Show and Tell. Bert could hardly wait for his turn.

Cookie Monster was first. He had brought his cookie cutter collection. He had large cookie cutters and small cookie cutters; he had square cookie cutters and round cookie cutters. He had Gingerbread Man, Santa Claus, and Easter Bunny cookie cutters.

Rodeo Rosie showed the class the lariat that her cousin Duane had brought her from Oklahoma. She could rope almost anything with that lariat.

Josie showed the class her new roller skates and skated in a figure eight.

Ernie paraded around the classroom to a marching beat that he played on his drum.

Herry Monster had brought his dancing shoes for Show and Tell. He demonstrated a leap that he had learned in dancing class.

Jamie went to his cubby hole to get what he had brought. It was a large pumpkin that he had helped his mother to grow.

At last it was Bert's turn. He hurried to his cubby to get his surprise for Show and Tell. But when Bert opened the box, it was empty! "Oh, no!" he wailed. "I brought a special surprise to share with you for Show and Tell—Bernice, my pet pigeon. But now she's gone, gone, *gone!*"

When they saw the empty box, they all began to look for Bernice.

"Don't worry, Bert. We'll find her," Betty Lou said. "Look! Pigeon tracks!" Sure enough, Bernice had walked across the wet paintings and left footprints all over the room!

Betty Lou followed the tracks along the art table...across the bookshelf...and into the play area.

"Ssh!" said Betty Lou. "I think I know where Bernice is!" She crept up to Herry's block castle...lifted up a block from the roof...and out flew Bernice!

"Bernice!" Bert cried, holding his arms out to her.

"Hey, she liked my castle," said Herry Monster.

"Catch her!" everyone yelled. But Bernice was scared by all the noise. She flew all around the room and no one could reach her.

Finally Bernice landed on a high shelf. "We'll never get her down!" cried Bert.

"Wait a minute!" Betty Lou said. "I think it's time for me to bring out the surprise *I* brought for Show and Tell."

"Show and Tell? At a time like *this*?" Bert moaned.

But Betty Lou was already opening her package. "It's peanut butter raisin bread that I made myself," she said proudly. "Be quiet, everybody, and let me try something."

Betty Lou sliced off a piece of bread and crumbled it onto the floor. She made a path of crumbs that led straight into Bernice's box.

Bernice saw the crumbs. She looked at them for what seemed like a very long time. Finally she hopped down from the shelf and started eating. Following the trail of crumbs, she ate and ate until she ate her way right back to her box.

"Bernice!" sighed Bert as he scooped her up.
"Your peanut butter raisin bread really did the trick,
Betty Lou!"

"How about a piece for you, Bert?" asked Betty
Lou. "And the next time we have Show and Tell,
why don't you leave Bernice at home and bring your
bottle cap collection instead?"

Lunchtime

It is lunchtime at school, but there are some things wrong with this picture! Can you find six silly things that don't belong in the school lunchroom?

Music Class

In music class we play instruments and sing.
Can you find these instruments in the picture below?

On the Playground

Everyone is playing hide-and-seek.
Ernie is "it." Can you help him find
Big Bird, Grover, Betty Lou, and Bert?

Clean Up Time

After art class, everyone helps
clean up the classroom.
What is Ernie doing?
What is Bert doing?
What is Grover doing?
What is Betty Lou doing?
What is Big Bird doing?

I liked it better
when it was messy!

SUPER-GROVER AND THE THREE BEARS

One day Grover went to the school auditorium to see the school play, "Goldilocks and the Three Bears." Prairie Dawn was playing the role of Goldilocks.

LOOK! THERE SHE IS! THAT IS MY FRIEND PRAIRIE DAWN!

SHHH! SHHH! SHHH! SHHH! SHHH! SHHH! SHHH!

In the play, Goldilocks ate up the bears' porridge and sat on the bears' chairs. Then she went and lay down on the bears' three beds.

"Oh, my," she said. "This bed is too hard. And this bed is too soft. But *this* bed is just *right*."

As soon as Goldilocks fell asleep on the little bear's bed, the three bears came home from their walk in the woods.

"Look, Daddy," said Herry Monster, who was playing the part of the baby bear in the school play. "There's a little girl sleeping in my bed. Yoo-hoo, little girl! Wake up."

Goldilocks sat up in bed and saw the three bears. "Oh!" she shrieked. "Bears! Oh, help! Three big terrible ferocious bears! Yeeek!"

"Oh, my goodness!" said Grover from the audience. "My friend Prairie Dawn is in a lot of trouble! Look at her screaming her head off up there. And no wonder. Just look at those bears! Why, those are three of the largest, meanest bears I have ever seen. They must have escaped from the zoo. I had better capture them. This is a job for . . . SUPER-GROVER!"

Grover jumped up from his seat. Then he thought of something important.

"Oh, dear," he said. "Oh, I am so embarrassed! I forgot that I must change into my Super-Grover costume before I can capture those horrible bears. Now, let me think. Ah, yes. I think I saw a telephone booth out in the lobby."

Grover quickly found the telephone booth and hurriedly changed into his Super-Grover costume.

"Boy," said Grover, "it sure is a good thing I remembered to put my cute little Super-Grover costume into the bottom of my lunchbox. You never can tell when it will come in handy."

Super-Grover rushed into the auditorium and leapt right onto the stage.

"Have no fear, Prairie Dawn!" he yelled. "Brave and fearless Super-Grover will take these three ugly and ferocious bears back to the zoo."

"Grover," said Prairie, "this is a *play*! Those are not real bears!"

With lightning speed, Super-Grover wrapped the three bears in a bedspread and flew up into the air, carrying them like a huge bundle of laundry.

"Do not worry, Prairie Dawn," said Super-Grover. "I will take care of these fierce bears so they will never bother you or anybody else again!"

And Super-Grover zoomed away through the open auditorium window.

He carried the three bears all the way to the zoo and lowered them into the big bear cage.

"There you are, back in the zoo," he said, "where big ferocious bears like you belong."

And then Super-Grover flew back to the school.

Back in the empty auditorium, Prairie Dawn sat all alone on the stage.

"I'll never forget what you did today, Grover," she said.

"Oh, do not thank me," he answered. "We super-heroes live to serve! Now that those three dangerous bears are back in the zoo, you can go on with your play."

Meanwhile, at the zoo . . .